This BOOK IS MADE of CLOUDS

MISHA MAYNERICK BLAISE

muddy boots

Guilford, Connecticut

An imprint of The Rowman & Littlefield Publishing Group, Inc.
4501 Forbes Blvd., Ste. 200
Lanham, MD 20706
www.rowman.com

MuddyBootsBooks.com

Distributed by NATIONAL BOOK NETWORK

British Library Cataloguing in Publication Information available

Library of Congress Control Number: 2020949149

ISBN 978-1-63076-388-6 (hardcover : alk. paper)
ISBN 978-1-63076-389-3 (electronic)

♾™ The paper used in this publication meets the minimum requirements of American National Standard for Information Sciences—Permanence of Paper for Printed Library Materials, ANSI/NISO Z39.48-1992.

Printed in Yuanzhou, China
February 2021

The whole universe has come together
to make your existence possible.

–Thich Nhat Hanh

So powerful is the light of unity
that it can illuminate the whole earth.

–Bahá'u'lláh

This BOOK is MADE OF CLOUDS.

Clouds stretch and change shape over mountains and seas.

Rain bursts from billowing clouds and falls upon forests below.
The trees grow and eventually they are used to make paper.

Forests are hidden inside of this book
and a cloud floats through every page.

Everything is connected to everything else.

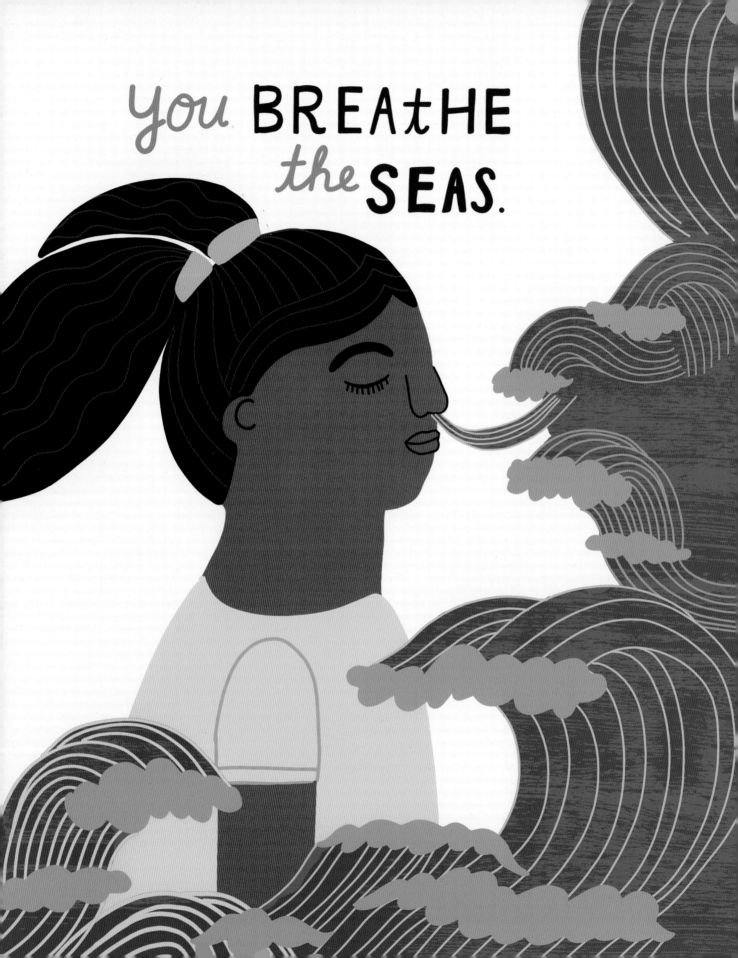

Living in the ocean are tiny creatures called phytoplankton. These creatures release half of the world's oxygen, including some of the oxygen that you are breathing right now.

Every time you inhale, a whale swims through your lungs and a sea horse kisses your nose.

Everything is connected to everything else.

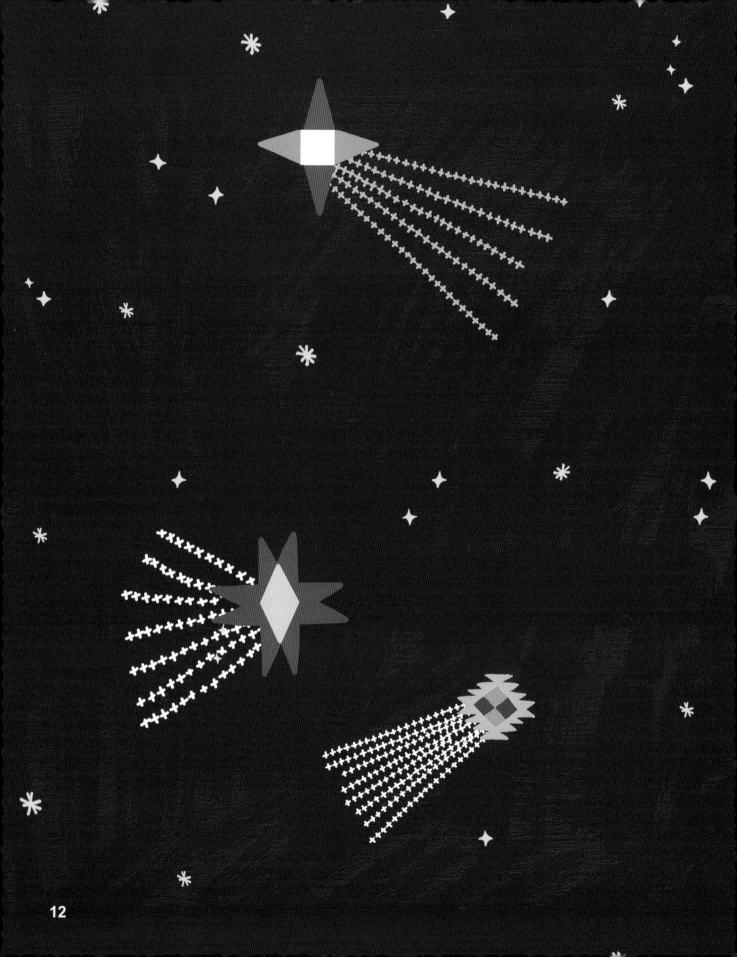

Billions of years ago, in the burning hearts of stars, new elements were created.

14

SUPERNOVAS EXPLODED!

The new elements that spread across space were some of the same elements that formed the Earth, and eventually created all life on our planet, including you.

The stars that illuminate the cosmos are your cousins, and all of Earth's creatures are your brothers and sisters.

16

Everything is connected to everything else.

you EAT
the SUN.

18

The beautiful burning sun bathes our planet in light, causing everything to grow. A plant catches a ray of the sun and turns that light into energy.

When you eat a plant, you eat that delicious energy that came from the sun.

The sun shines inside of you, and plants thread through your hair. Everything is connected to everything else.

THE EARTH is YOUR HOME.

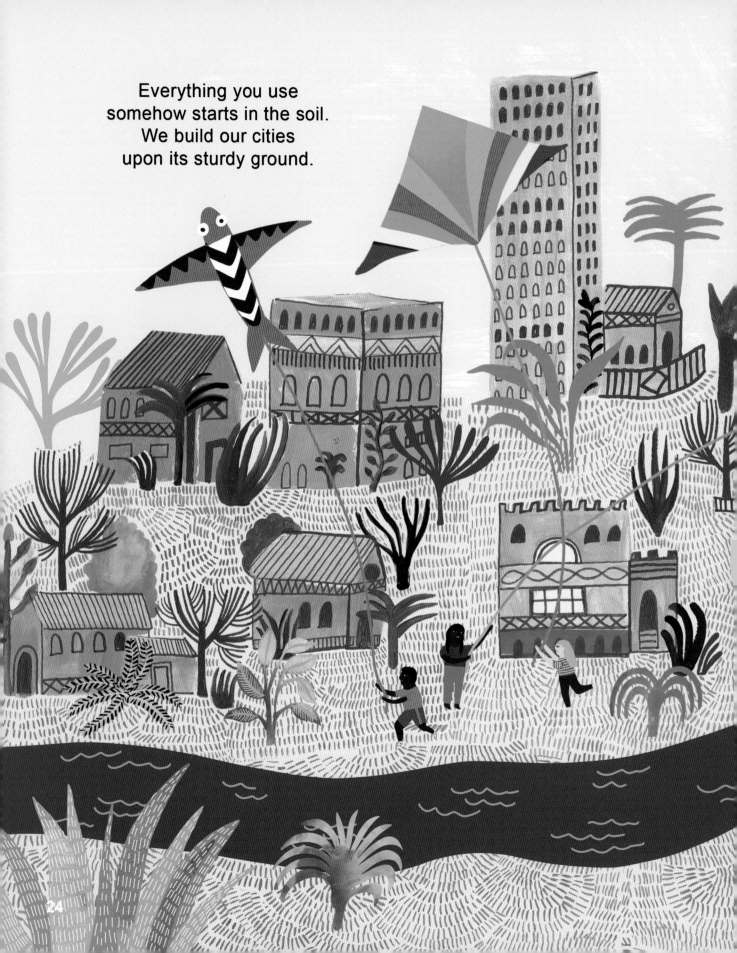

Everything you use
somehow starts in the soil.
We build our cities
upon its sturdy ground.

24

Soil catches rain and snow, creating wild rivers whose waters eventually enter pipes and flow into your home.

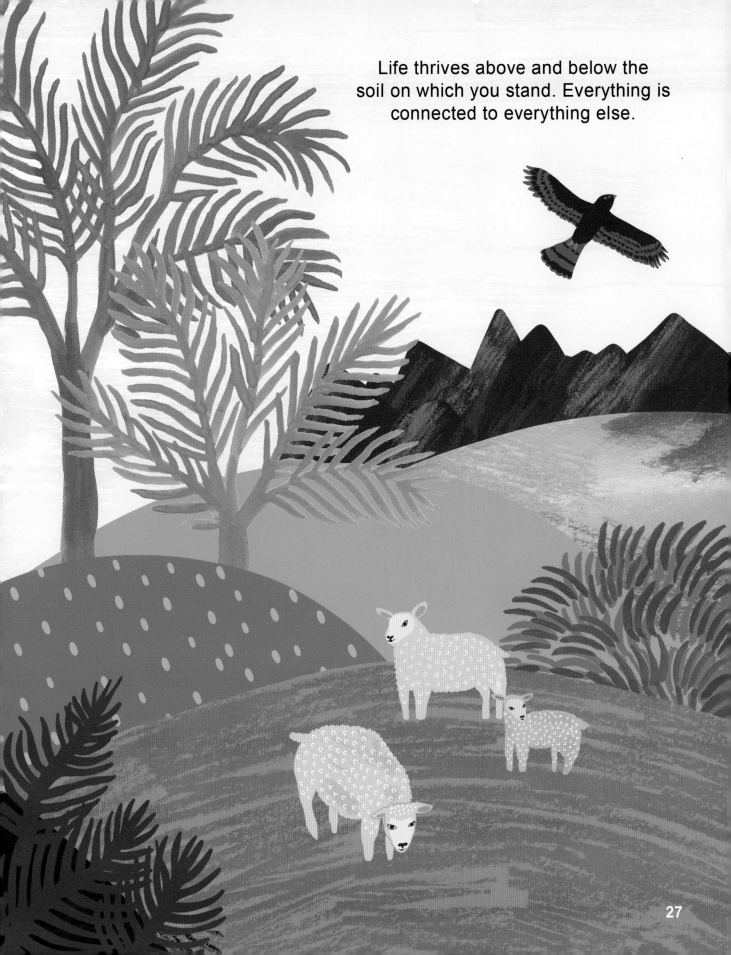

Life thrives above and below the soil on which you stand. Everything is connected to everything else.

WE ARE ONE HUMAN FAMILY.

We are all related as distant cousins.
All of us are very different, and also we
are very much the same.

We are born from the stars and supported by the sun, water, forests, soil, and clouds.

We are the leaves of one tree.

EVERYONE IS
CONNECtED to
EVERYONE
ELSE.

ACtiVitiES

PLANt MEDItAtION

Spend some time mindfully observing a plant or a tree. You don't have to be in the middle of a forest. It's okay to find a plant that's growing in a city!

Observe the plant with all of your senses (except taste . . . don't eat it!). Look carefully and try to observe small details. Touch it gently and discover its texture. Smell and see if it emits a scent. Listen and see if it makes a sound, like leaves shaking in the breeze.

Take a few deep breaths and sit quietly with the plant. Feel the presence of the plant and remember that it's a living being just like you. Reflect on how you and the plant are both connected to air, water, soil, and the sun.

NAtURE MANDALA

A creative way to connect with nature is to make a mandala on the ground using found elements. A mandala is basically a geometric design around a center point. Create your design using things like pinecones, shells, rocks, or twigs. Enjoy the process of creating art outside—you can't take it with you!

Or, try making nature faces!

THE EARTH IS YOUR HOME ART ACtIVItY

Materials: paper, markers, and crayons

Pages 22 to 23 show a house made out of earthly elements. Try drawing your own Earth home. Each room can have different people, creatures, animals, plants, or landforms that are part of our planet.

ONE HUMAN FAMILY
GROUP ACTIVITY

Materials: one ball of yarn

This activity is a tangible way to imagine the connections that unite us.

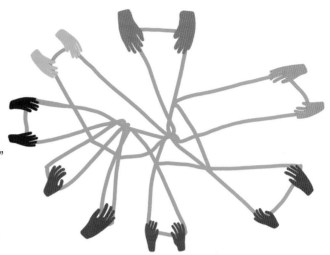

The first person holding the ball of yarn shares a positive quality about themselves (e.g., "I am kind," "I am good at sharing," "I'm a hard worker," "I'm encouraging," etc.). They will hold on to the end of the string and throw the ball to another participant across the circle. Continue this way until each person is holding a piece of string and a web has formed between everyone.

Invite participants to gently tug at the string to see how everyone is connected. Share with them that the string represents how, as one human family, we always impact each other. Our positive qualities can be used to uplift and support each other. Invite one person to drop their piece of string to show how if anyone is excluded from the human family, the support system becomes slack and not as strong.

In the end, cut the yarn into pieces and tie a yarn bracelet around each participant's wrist as a reminder of how we are always connected to one another.

ONE HUMAN FAMILY ART ACTIVITY

Pages 28 to 29 show many diverse members of the human race. When you understand that you are part of one human family, you will care about, respect, and value the other people who share this world with you.

Draw a picture of a child from a culture different from your own, and illustrate something you could do together as friends. For example, you could share some ice cream, play soccer together, dance, invent a new machine, or fly kites.

MISHA MAYNERICK BLAISE

Misha Maynerick Blaise is an artist and illustrator known for her bold use of color and compelling designs. She also likes to write about how we are interconnected with everyone and everything. Her most recent books, *This Phenomenal Life* (Lyons Press) and *Crazy for Birds*, remind us of our enduring connection with nature and our astonishing relationship with the whole universe. She currently lives with her husband and two sons in Northwest Arkansas.